FINISHING LINE PRESS
www.finishinglinepress.com

Thunder in the Courtyard:
Kajari Poems

poems by

Rajiv Mohabir

Finish Line Press
Georgetown, Kentucky

Thunder in the Courtyard:
Kajari Poems

ACKNOWLEDGMENTS

Editor: Christen Kincaid

Cover Art: "Megha Mallar Raga, Foloi from Ragamala *(Garland of Melodies)*
LACMA M.71.1.24" is licensed under CC BY 2.0

Author Photo: Charmila Ajmera

Cover Design: Elizabeth Maines

Printed in the USA on acid-free paper.
Order online: www.finishinglinepress.com
                 also available on amazon.com

Author inquiries and mail orders:
Finishing Line Press
P. O. Box 1626
Georgetown, Kentucky 40324
U. S. A.

Table of Contents

for Jordan Andrew Miles

शुक्ला पक्ष
Bright Fortnight

Raga: मेघ मल्हार

समय: To be sung at night during the monsoon

Scale:

Ascending: S m R m P n S'

(मोर, कपोत, सांड, कपोत, कोयल, हाथी, मोर)

ताल: Jhap

आज पिया जायेगा विदेश
समन्दर मेरा नमक निगलेगा।

रे पानी की लहर,

मेरे किनारे से उसके किनारे तक
मेरी दुआ ले पहुँचाना।

Today my love leaves me;
the sea will drink my salt.

O wave,

from my shore to his
carry my du'a.

Sajana,

Wind shakes me   awake.

At midnight I call out
but my house
            is empty.

I clip my toenails past the bed,
even this body   is hollow.

The house is a metaphor
                for the body,
how literal must I be?

                Where is outside
where is inside?

            I call out   for you
but my house

        is empty.

तृतीय

Sajana,

I pluck a weeping cuckoo
            from the branch

and with one bite
     its breast   is a poisoned apple.

I pull feathers from my mouth,
         down sticking the throat.

Your song bleeds
       from my chest.

How can a monsoon bird
        prick the heart
        once swallowed?

What is this flutter
     against my ribs,

        this relentless sting?

चतुर्थी

A distant koyal
strikes one note
in three octaves.

   Piya.

      Piya.

         Piya.

Sajana,

You send a photo:
a plastic grey whale—
                    a cetacean
that returns
        to California each summer.

From Waimea I imagine you
standing   on some Santa Barbara beach.
Your footprints
            fill with rain.

Radha drowns Krishna's prints
in her salt. His only sound
a ghost:
        his reed flute's blue wail.

षषठी

बिदेस से केसरवा भेजेला बलमवा
पिया तू ना जाने

केसरवा किसून के रंगवा
उही जे रधिया के छोड़ देले

जमुना के तीर भीगल गइल
तोहारे बाँसुरी के बेला से।

My love sends saffron from afar.
Piya, don't you know

saffron is Krishna's color,
the same Krishna who left Radha

on the Jamuna's banks, soaked
in the spell of your flute?

सप्तमी

Sajana,

After night's monsoon
the morning's silence unsettles.

Last night:
        your voice in symphony;
at dawn:
        a double bar.

Day's body is empty:
        all black notes lift from the staff

as swallows in heat. All instruments
refuse their strumming
                        without hands

guiding rivers from their bells. I am
a flute with no one

                to press out
                        my song.

अष्टमी
(

Rain,
		do not kick up dust.

				O, dusk cloud,

Do not stir

		his memory.

नवमी
(

Sajana,

Apart,
      the ocean
           and sky pant

for the other's lips.

Clouds erupt
         from craving.

In the hot months
     your absence
           is like thirst:

so unmovable
     and yet so moving.

दशमी
(

Sajana,

Since you left
            I've not touched

your side of our bed,
        leaving   space

            for where you belong.

In a dream I hear
        your voice—

so soothing, yet
            stoking fire.

एकादशी
(

Sajana,

Come sunrise I regret
I can't pin my dream of you

on its back, and press my brow
into its nape nor drink

your body's scent before you wake:
that at dawn you are a shadow

erased by light.

द्वादशी
(

झींगुर ने अपना कला शुरू कर लिया
नमी पार काट रहा है उसका गाना
कैसे काटूंगा समय पलंग पर लेटा
बिना तेरे?

झींगुर सिर्फ तेरा नाम जपता है
तेरी गीली याद से भला कैसे सूखा?
कोइ चौरा नहीं
तेरे नाम में डूबने छोड़कर।

The cricket begins his night-art,
his song cuts through humidity.

How to endure the night
                on this bed
without you?

He keeps chanting your name.
Soaked in you,
                how will I ever dry?

There is no other road
                but to drown.

त्रयोदशी
(

Raven wings, the cloud's
enveloping scale.

Moon orbs, emeralds on
the blades of grass.

Moist copper
incense: pine needles
in rain.

Humid dusk music.

Treefrogs, throats
swell dark hours,
long for the other.

In which month will you return?

चतुर्दशी

Sajana,

The sky and sea fuck.
This is why

        monsoons drive you mad;
the blood's salt burns hot.

On the shore, a sudden torrent.

Come back.

      Out this blaze.

पूर्णिमा
(Full Moon)
○

हम अभी अभी पयलिया बान्धे
अउर तू गहरी नदिया के पार गइला

महेंदी उतर जाये अउर तोहार
कोई भी निसनवा नाहीं रहे

I have just fastened my anklets
and you have crossed the deep river.

My mehendi fades and soon
no trace of you will remain.

कृष्णा पक्ष
Dark Fortnight

Raga: मेघ मल्हार

समय: To be sung at night during the monsoon

Scale:

अवरोहण: सा' निश़ प म रे सा रे ,निश़ सा

      (peacock, elephant, nightingale, dove, bull, dove, peacock)

ताल: Jhap

एगो कोकिला निगली ताकी
पिठवा से पंख उगाईहे अउर हम
बिरह के आसूँ पीअत है
इ नीमकहरमवा के
पता चलल कि चिड़िया नाहीं
हम सँपवा पालत रही
जिगरवा पर बैठके
पसलिया के पिंजरवा से
तोहार कजरिया सुनावत रहेला
इ कम्बख़्त कोयलिया

I swallowed a kokila so
wings would sprout from my back;
I gave it to drink anguish.
This traitorous thing
wasn't a bird at all,
come to find out.
This whole time
I had raised a snake
that sits on my heart
and sings from my breast
your *kajari*, your monsoon
songs,
this cursed bird.

द्वितय

)

Sajana,

Swells shadow-puppet
          dolphin shapes in the bay.

You are painted   on my sheets
the color of Krishna,   of illusion:
      the empty
              behind the shape;

a midnight storm head, your ruckus
refuses to let me sleep; the streak

of kohl on Radha's
              deserted cheek.

तृतीय
)

Sajana,

Bamboo shards float
    down
        every stream
            I cross.

As I walk   splinters stick
my feet,
    my palms,
        my eyes.

Somewhere inside
    your music
    will not stop—

will I never be rid of you?

चतुर्थी
)

The gully is a swollen river.

Rain overflows the temple pond.

>   *rim*
>   *jhim*

>   *rim*
>   *jhim*

>   *rim*
>   *jhim*

Drops are diamonds set in eye wells.

>   *Piya, which road has swallowed your feet?*

सतरंग के राम धनुसवा
    कहइलस जाइला
काहेकि सावन
       के महिनवा में

बिना तोहार
    बरसात का हर एगो
रिमझिम रिमझिम
      ख़तरनाक तीर

बन जाइला अउर
    इ बेसहारा दिल
सिकारी के निसान वाला
      भागत हिरण बनेला।

They call the rainbow
    "Ram's bow"
because in the month
    of Saavan,

without you,
    the rain's every
rim-jhim rim-jhim
      is a poisoned

arrow and this
    helpless heart
is a fleeing deer.

षषठी

)

Sajana,

Your imprint fills my heart
with dark,
   my throat
   with holes.

There's no need
   to take a flame
to hollow a reed, my bed
is sick   with night.

How useless
to be an opening, a thing
    of neither place.

What good is a reed
   without a shehenai?

How useless I am
   without you.

सप्तमी
◗

Sajana,

It took me years
          to realize
this body is a beena.

See the holes?   Here
is the hollow
          where your breath goes,

put your fingers   here to start
and stop   the flow.
                    This

is where your lips
      are meant to go.
                    That's why

the beena maker carved it.

अष्टमी

◗

अब ना बजावो श्याम बाँसुरया
तरसे लेगेला सावन के विरानिया

Krishna, do not play your flute;
the loneliness of Saavan begins its ache.

नवमी

Sajana,

You're gone, so
    I threw away

every last reed
    I could find.

If I play this raga
    the monsoon will never end.

Why does the wooden lilt
    creep into my head

as blood
    circling my ear?

दशमी

●

Sajana,

I've taken to smashing flutes
with my hands and feet;

throwing them out won't do.
Some ghost finds them at night

and keeps me sweating in my sheets.

My friends now call me
Bamboo Smasher—

Imagine the panic in Kane'ohe,
a town named "Bamboo Man"

when they hear you've gone.

एकादशी
●

Sajana,

Your ghost is a splinter
made from what I love:

     a trace of misery and music
that juts from my finger,

a shard of the flute
     I put to my lips:

     what once soothed the blood
but stirred the feet

now aches;
     now stabs.

द्वादशी

Wind shaken leaves,

        melody swells

   twelve

     love stories

        high.

Breeze—

           do not play. Do not play.
           Flute stream, do not flood.

●

Sajana,

Like stars,   I string my tears
as pearls to count each
                    smooth star
in this constellation of want—

one hundred eight beads on the mala
strung with torn bedclothes.
                    Each bead

a bleary prayer,   each pearl an hour
spent without you,   each hour
a wraith   of your perfume.

Listless,
        my eyes are bloodshot.
When will you come to lend
                    an hour of relief?

I am a raw vessel.

Play a beat on my clay lip:

    dhum dhum
        dhum dhum

      Thunder in courtyard

    dhum dhum
        dhum dhum

my body is this
un-fashioned earth.

Piya, come.
      Get your hands dirty.

अमावस्या
(New Moon)
●

सजनवा मारो ना नजरिया
तोहार अखिया के तीरवा से
ना हमार हिरदय तोड़ा

सुरहिया फ़टके भीगाई हमार वेस
बदनिया फ़टके हाँस उड़ जाई कउन देस

साइँया मारो ना नजरिया
तोहार अखिया के गोलिया से
जिउ हमार जड़ जाईहे

Sajana, don't look at me.
With your eyes
don't stick my heart.

My clay pot will break,
          soaking my clothes.

This body will break;
          no telling where
                    this swan will fly.

Saiya, don't look at me so,
from your stare

                    my life is lost.

CPSIA information can be obtained
at www.ICGtesting.com
Printed in the USA
LVHW042258270119
605466LV00001B/206/P